4:30 MOVIE

Also by Donna Masini

That Kind of Danger

About Yvonne

Turning to Fiction

4:30 MOVIE

POEMS

Donna Masini

W. W. NORTON & COMPANY
Independent Publishers Since 1923
New York | London

For information about permission to reproduce selections from this book,
write to Permissions, W. W. Norton & Company, Inc.,
500 Fifth Avenue, New York, NY 10110

For information about special discounts for bulk purchases, please contact
W. W. Norton Special Sales at specialsales@wwnorton.com or 800-233-4830

Manufacturing by Versa Press
Production manager: Julia Druskin

Library of Congress Cataloging-in-Publication Data

Names: Masini, Donna, author.
Title: 4:30 movie : poems / Donna Masini.
Other titles: Four thirty movie
Description: First Edition. | New York : W. W. Norton & Company, [2018] |
Includes bibliographical references.
Identifiers: LCCN 2018004875 | ISBN 9780393635508 (hardcover)
Classification: LCC PS3563.A7855 A6 2018 | DDC 811/.54—dc23
LC record available at https://lccn.loc.gov/2018004875

W. W. Norton & Company, Inc., 500 Fifth Avenue, New York, N.Y. 10110
www.wwnorton.com

W. W. Norton & Company Ltd., 15 Carlisle Street, London W1D 3BS

1 2 3 4 5 6 7 8 9 0

In memory of my sister
Karen Weinstein

;

for my brother
David Masini

Contents

;

;

Acknowledgments

Thanks to the following publications in which these poems first appeared:

Academy of American Poets Poem-a-Day: "A Gate"; *Best American Poetry*: "Anxieties" (originally in *Academy of American Poets Poem-a-Day*); *Cortland Review*: "Movie"; *H.O.W.*: "A Fable," "Trying to Understand Irony," "Watching the Six-Part *Pride and Prejudice,* Mid-Chemo, with My Sister"; *Ploughshares*: "Waiting Room"; *Poetry*: "Mind Screen"; *Provincetown Arts*: "Tracking Shot: Subway Lines"; *Referential*: "Revolve," "Storylines"; *SITES: Translating Trump*: "The Blob"; *Village Voice*: "The Lights Go Down at the Angelika"

;

Thank you Marie Howe, Jan Heller Levi, Catherine Barnett and Kim Addonizio for your steady spirits, poem by poem.

For thoughtful readings and suggestions, thank you Mark Doty, Michael Klein, Medrie MacPhee, Daniel Mendelsohn, Honor Moore, Brittany Perham, Robert Polito, Victoria Redel, Martha Rhodes, James Stoeri and Alexander Stille.

Thank you Ghislaine Boulanger, Roger Celestin, Elisa D'Arrigo, Lynne Greenberg, Gail Hochman, Walter Mosley, Karen Backus, Stephen Simcock, and Drew Weitman.

Jill Bialosky, once again, so much gratitude.

To Civitella Ranieri, *grazie, grazie, grazie*.

Love and gratitude to my parents, to Paul Weinstein and Mallory Kusterer; and to Ryan, for the joy you brought us in a terrible time.

Deleted Scene: Worry (.14)

(Living Room: Interior)

All these years, my sister says,
worrying something would happen.
And now it has.

;

The Lights Go Down at the Angelika

and you press into the dark, imagine
the stranger two rows back, that fragile
chance you'll forget in the second trailer.

Now it's quiet, still
this burden of being watcher and screen
and what floats across it—light pouring out

its time and necklines and train wrecks.
What a relief to yield to the EXIT
sign red "I" blinking like a candle.

Soon the enormous figures moving
across rooms, the emphatic narrative
arcs. (There's the thrum of the subway,

its engine of extras.) Here now
the beginning of trivia tests. Warning puppets
with brown-bag faces and fringy hair.

You're almost here. But what you want
is the *after*. How yourself you are now
walking into the night, full moon over Houston Street,

at the bright fruit stand touching the yellow
mums. Here you are: Woman With Cilantro
listening to the rattle of the wrap,

the paper sound paper makes after you
have heard movie paper. Apples are more *apples*.
Paper more *paper*. Cilantro, its sweaty green self.

Waiting Room

My sister's inside in a green gown
and I'm here twisting dread into origami
tissues, riot mind ticking *wrong wrong*.
Is this what's been waiting
all along? All of us carried off on a train,
pressed to a window, charting the crazy migration
of cells, disaster oaring
steadily after us like Magi
to the babe. And time, grim monitor,
screening each of us in our green toga.
One day you're drinking your first martini,
a minute later you're roaming
some hospital wing. (Why call it a wing?
Why say origami when it's a useless rag?)
Now none of it matters. My iron
will, impeccable timing.
I think of a far-off war-torn town
hiding my sister in her twin gown.

Mind Screen

It's a kind of crime scene,
as if the mind were a dime
novel, a scrim of need and semen,
all cinder and siren, a dim
prison where the miser dines
on rinds of desire, and the sinner,
sincere as denim, repeats Eden's
demise—that luckless toss of dice.
Yet here at the rim of this demesne
a mitigating *mise-en-scène*:
a close-up of her mother stirring rice,
a glass of sparkling cider, a mince
pie spliced in— not to rescind or mend:
what mind denies mercies mine in the end.

Pronoun Problem

Watch yourself, your mother
used to say. Watch
what you're doing. Watch
your mouth. There you are:
a girl with pink chewing gum.
You're three. There's the fire escape.
Your sister is being born.
Your uncle is keeping an eye on you.
Watch the way you talk
to yourself. Your nothing
is never as good as her nothing.
Whoever she is.

Tracking Shot: Subway (Interior)

Bad things tend to happen quickly
the doctor said last week, meaning to comfort.
So many shopping bags. Paper or plastic, the weary cashiers ask.
People who bought this also bought . . .
Particles like Grape-Nuts rain over Paris.
The long ramble into _____. And the tests that come
every night. Sometimes the test's called *Where's My Bag?* Sometimes
Find the Hidden _____. So many forms. In case of emergency
. . . date of last . . . Frame the question. Make a scene.
A story is like an eye chart. Better this way or [lens flips] this way.
This way or [lens flips]

Watching the Six-Part *Pride and Prejudice*, Mid-Chemo, with My Sister

We start stopping when she's afraid
something bad will happen. Don't worry,
I say, all will be well.

How could she know? She's never
read it, never heard of Elizabeth
and Jane, never wanted Mr. Darcy. Like me

she needs to know how things will end.
I know Elizabeth will be fine. As I knew,
last week, my sister weeping, that Elinor—

sobbing, begging—wouldn't lose Marianne.
It's Jane Austen! My sister doesn't know that
in Austen nothing really bad happens. I leave her

on the couch with the last hours.
How much my sister will have to endure,
alone, with this new drama.

Later her message. The last one
in which she will sound like herself.
Hi, it's me. The movie was unbelievable.

Unbelievable.

What Didn't Work

Chemo   Tarceva   prayer
meditation   affirmation   Xanax
Avastin   Nebulizer   Zofran
Zoloft   Vicodin   notebooks
nurses   oxygen tank   pastina
magical thinking   PET scans   movies
therapy   phone calls   candles
acceptance   denial   meatloaf
doctors   rosary beads   sleep
Irish soda bread   internet   incantations
visitors   sesame oil   pain patches
CAT scans   massage   shopping
thin sliced Italian bread with melted mozzarella
St. Anthony oil   Lourdes water   St. Peregrine
tea   spring water   get well cards
relaxation tapes   recliner   cooking shows
cotton T-shirts   lawn furniture   a new baby
giving up Paris   giving up Miami   charts
bargaining   not bargaining   connections
counting with her   breathing for her   will
Pride and Prejudice   Downton Abbey   prayer
watching TV   not watching TV   prayer
prayer   prayer   prayer
lists

The Extra

Once again she's reading about impermanence, pencil in hand, starring the parts she's marked before.

Her script asks her to think of a wave: *seen one way it seems to have distinct identity*, in another, it's *just the behavior of water.* She underlines this.

Empty of identity but full of water, her script says, *temporarily possible . . . a set of constantly changing behaviors.* She underlines this, too.

Sometimes she reads a headline and feels like she's in a car with a crazed erratic driver—feet braced against the dashboard. (The Krebs cycle cycling inside her, but she can't remember what it does.)

She likes the phrase "interior silence" but thinks she's only experienced this while sick in bed with a fever.

Now she's practicing seeing death everywhere—on the subway: each corpse looking into a cell phone screen. Some corpses are wearing expensive boots. Watches.

Her script says it is absolutely certain we are to die, and that she is supposed to believe this.

Rehearsing a commercial for SoulCycle she is trying to see people as waves. Grief comes in waves. And light. And the rolling dust-motes in her childhood bedroom. And roll.

She and her sister wanted waves. They pinned rollers to their heads, stiff bristles like artificial Christmas trees, digging into their scalps as they slept. Their hair was straight, limp as prayer book pages. Waves didn't last. Their mother decided to give them permanents.

Still pedaling the stationary bicycle she can't stop thinking about the village that fell asleep for one hundred years and everything—the broom mid-sweep! water pouring from the pitcher!—stayed the same.

So many people creeping around inside what they label her "petite ethnic-type" self on the back of her headshot.

The torture reports . . . cops shooting the unarmed . . . How to pick out the one displaced face that lets her imagine millions. What is her role?

Every wave related to every other wave, her script says. She's rarely been in a close-up. Mostly pans, tracking shots.

Here they've marked her place by a pond, her brother saying *this won't end well*. Her backstory sister teaching her to deadhead the roses.

When she has no list of things to do, she is listless.

We die alone but we go to the movies together, she writes in her journal. Bye-bye! her mother waves in the 8mm home movie. *Wave goodbye girls.* And cut.

A jazzy labyrinth from labia to grave, she writes.

There it is: childhood gone. That Old Brooklyn with its clotheslines and yellow fallout shelter signs. (Rice Krispies snap crackle and popping in the turquoise plastic bowls.)

Hers is a small part and she knows no one's watching, still she is sincere and carries her intention. She thinks of this at the protest march with her red-markered RESIST rag pinned to her coat collar.

She rearranges the letters on a movie poster in the oncologist's office and finds St. Anthony. She thinks this means everything will be ok.

She thinks what's the difference between prayer and worry?

Even when she *watches* a movie she imagines herself as one of the faceless victims falling into a clump of leaves . . . In a crowd of refugees creeping along the edges of the screen.

Secretly she thinks of certain Chinese films in which what is *really* important appears at the edge.

She has never gotten past a wave in any ocean. Once she was knocked unconscious by the behavior of water.

She knows her most important moments will be in deleted scenes.

A Fable

Driving into the heart of night we arrive at the part
of the movie where I start tap-dancing, tap-tapping
across a tin sheet, a sort of surfing airborne pan

listing side to side, and me, tilting to
balance, announcing I am Esther Williams.
All is blue, salty with prayer and incantation,

all dazzling aristocratic hands. But it wasn't the heart
of night. There was no heart. It was true
about the tilting, but the movie not a movie at all,

just the usual drivel and sludge, and never having seen
Esther Williams, in truth I'd only conjured
a wet black forties one-piece and rubber bathing cap.

Oh what's the use. It's grief's freeze-frame churchyard
with its fresh cut dirge, its pretend heaven. Watch me
driving myself down this winding country road, top down,

one hand on the wheel, the other grabbing back my thick blond hair
like some Monica Vitti whose leopard kerchief the wind sucked off
long ago. Hours? Decades? Now, wanting a bit of *chachacha*,

she flips the radio dial loosing a grassy static,
a spasmodic numbing hive-buzz of stumbling bees.
She flips it off. She'll be drifting in that static soon enough

with her ballet flats and tin rigor mortis. *Allora! In bocca al lupo*
cries a child's nightlight, while night releases its indifferent stars.

Anxieties

It's like ants
and more ants.

West, east
their little axes

hack and tease.
Your sins. Your back taxes.

This is your Etna,
your senate

of dread, at the axis
of reason, your taxi

to hell. You see
your past tense—

and next? a nest
of jittery ties.

You're ill at ease,
at sea,

almost in-
sane. You've eaten

your saints.
You pray to your sins.

Even sex
is no exit.

Ah, you exist.

Hell

The first time I saw the word, the helpless guppy "e"
stuck between the stern black bars, my catechism
darkened, and forced to write a page of "I," I

crammed those thick lead marks across my composition
book until it looked like a prison, emblem of my recalcitrance,
the fences I'd have to jump to rid my pencil self of sin,

and saw the place I'd surely end: unkempt, my disobedience
marked in the Hormel Dark Canned Ham on the butcher's shelf I
imagined was the shape of my soul. Is it inside me, my Interior

Castle, as I lie here *bang bang bang bang* in this MRI
that began as gentle small-town mending and turned
to coffin laughter. What disaster is it pounding out as I

wander in the sound, amorphous as water, strapped to a board,
technicians sliding me out and in like a sequined lady in a magic act
(green smock, hairnet, booties) sawed in half, reassembled

in her bassinet of tricks—*Voilà*! Hello! Hello! I'm back!
Will it reveal itself, that canned black ham, lodged in my rib cage?
Oh soul. Oh God to petition and plead. Oh Hormel.

The word was "Hell," and I the helpless guppy in its cage.
Not the first time I knew words were fishes, but this was a burned
barred voice, all traps and tentacles. Hell, I'm seeing cages

everywhere. My new cats shrieking in their black mesh tent,
pressed to my bed. Like living with my future tomb.
Last night one escaped, clung to the tent head like a weathervane,

its yowling fur porcupining out. Let it represent my pain: eluding
doctors, X-rays, squatting in my body, knocking over bowls
as if it moved in one grim night (oh God what a zoo!)

a jaw clamp pain that will not let a screech squeak through.
Teeth-grinding rages. It is said grief comes in stages. In this it's
like cancer, like Comedies and Tragedies, apartments that are tough to

sell until they're dolled up to trick a buyer. *Almost over*, the technician
says. Goodbye! Goodbye! God of my childhood. I'm sliding
out of your hood of pall. Goodbye last journal, wretched parentheses,

awful grieving sentences in which my sister died,
my two cats, sister's dog, niece's dog, brother's dog.
Goodbye diary of the time all hell broke loose—and

nothing can get it back in its cage.

Deleted Scene: Diagnosis (.23)

(Kitchen: Interior)

First they said allergy, then we worried.
Now she's on the phone with the doctor, motions:
Thumbs Up! Haha, we say. Thumb cancer!
She hangs up. Pneumonia. Hooray!
Pleurisy and pneumonia! Such old-fashioned diseases.
But we'll take them.

The Port

When the veins give out they stick in a port.
She rewraps the thin gown they gave out,
lets phantom chance chart the range in the next report
as blood draws its inevitable decimals.
Once I imagined the cave a soul makes to house spirit,
plush dusk where a girl might hide her hectic book,
her portal into the thrum of what would vein her song.

Movie

My mother is scissoring strips of paper bag, fringing
the edges, stapling layers of feathery brown to an old jacket,

then, rings glinting on her wedding finger, whisks
the scissor up each ribbon of fringe, tricks it to curl, to turn

my brother into an owl. It's fall in the late sixties. She zips him in.
Cut now to this other fall. Invisible

exclamation points shooting through everything:
Wind! Trees! Shaky mums! The city's *lousy* with academics

a man on Houston Street says to what appears to be his date.
Suddenly it's cold to dine outside. In the window of Paradise Thai

two women lean across a flickering candle, glasses of bright wine.
A chilly tableau framed by night, a lustrous couple

of inscrutable statues, pineapple crowns rising into spires. At this point
everything is still possible. I wish they could see this. Moonlit spires.

Their lustrous doubles. Every time, every *single* time I've followed desire,
my friend said last night, pressing her palms on my kitchen table, *every* time,

disaster. It's late. The babysitter will be fifty dollars.
Moon! Time! Fifty dollars! What an expensive movie.

Sometimes we walk out of ourselves, blinking into the light,
pulling our sweaters tighter, unprotected, regressed from our time

in the dark, the crowd snaking through the lobby, eager to enter
what we have left. We're always waiting for the next thing

to change us. Facelifts, my ex-husband said last week, a new cure
for migraine. Light flickered its misty nimbus, his face breaking up.

I held my head. Jews have over twenty-five words for *schmo*, I said,
apropos of nothing. After so much pain, imagine, we can laugh.

Though if you think in anagrams, parades and drapes, diapers, rape,
despair and aspire all come out of paradise.

What was my mother thinking as she made my brother an owl,
as an ordinary man and woman leaned toward one another

at a railway station table, away from their marriages, across our TV screen
entering the movie, heading into, then averting, perhaps, disaster. Perhaps.

We *feel* change coming. Season of exclamation points.
Fringy mums shaking their yellow frazzle!

Last week, still summer, a young attendant in the designer jeans store
held out our change, announced the world will end in _____.

Might as well, he said, keep drinking the plastic
bottles of Poland Spring. Well, it's a doggy-dog world

as my sister says. My friend throws up her arms,
waves her free alterations. Look how much we've done

in just a few minutes! Look how we wait
for something to change us: love, jeans, a "Train of Thought"

hanging in the subway car: *As Gregor Samsa awoke one morning from uneasy dreams he found himself transformed*, etc.

What did he dream? Did we find out?
Why remember the creature but not the dream?

What was my brother thinking as he flapped and whoo'd across that stage? *Whoo whoo whoo*, he hooted for days.

Storylines

He was fond of phrases like "the grim reaper"—the very thing
not to say the night he picked up the skinny hitchhiker
is the kind of story you can make up in thirty seconds, conjuring

a riot of possibility and violence, two unnamed—ok, call them
Harry and Larry and imagine there's a place
for these potential extras, mindlessly invented, suspended

in a kind of protoplasmic limbo Dante knew something about.
They haven't done anything yet, but lie mewing in their bluish onesies
beside the social worker who met the foster parent in a gritty café.

(He was covered in cat hair, something she'd later tell the police.)
What happens to these people we keep making up? I like to think of them
incubating in an adjacent world—*Inciting Incidents, Abandoned Drafts*—

where one cop begins to have a body. Overweight. White. Significant
Details poisoning his mother's cats with random eucalyptus.
Invention is reckless. Or do they exist before we pluck them

from their yeasty ether, eager to nurse them, foster, pet, and send them off
in the hope they'll rise and . . . Sometimes I wonder about the infinite.
So many words. Endless combinations. So why so hard

to sit in this dreaded plenitude increasing the population?
I can't even think of a name for my cat.

"Gone Girl"

What twist of puppet-strung manipulations gone
wrong, what jerked-up dumb show, know-nothing, nothing

but strings jerking on strings, unloved, over-governed, outline plotted
dolls hog-tied to other dolls, stringing them along, egging them on,

what short-order mannequins and blood-drenched negligees.
Want to know what's gone? My sister's dead. *That's* gone.

And this jerry-rigged pretender no more heart
than a seven-year ball of rubber bands is a soul.

What is prayer but a rigged-up jerking doll hefting
its measly petitions—*don't let her die, don't let her die*—heaving over

and over our over-willed stillborn over-determined begging.
When it's over and the nauseous credits roll what's gone

is time. Gone the girl praying to the puppeteer. That girl
strung out on prayer. She's gone.

;

Water Lilies

for Karen

Water Lilies 1

Here the weariest

          come to rest

                 in the swirl

     of light and time and water

             water and air

                 blues, teals

   a twisting wisteria

            seems to wrestle

    the trellis

        of its own trail

                  tier on tier

   climbing its wires

          of air

       After the war

   in his atelier

        a fog, a silt

            filming each iris

  Monet twisted the laws

       of landscape and paint to raise

    the real

      into a kind of stairwell

           to tease

    his Parisians out of the sterile

trials of war

      to rest

        not to erase

  but ease

      let them stare

         and stare

Water Lilies 2

trying to sit

                        at the rail

         of my attention, wait

                  (what can I take for later?)

(in the bookstore, retail

              retail!)

                          (outside the swelter)

      six hours behind me my sister lies

                  in a tangle of wires

            and sweat

                  can't eat, then rallies, tires

        In a week I'll

             open a book: Art

             I'll give her Art

prayer, the clinical trials

             and all

        will

              be well

                all

will be   all

            will will will

               too late

in a year she will

         (this can't be real)

             Later

when I buy myself a sweater

           I buy one for her as well

Water Lilies 3

        After the allies

               after the serial

                            trials

the lies

       his real

             aim was to make a

     "pond that remembers all"

                     not to paint "it"

     rather "the air

             that touched it"

Water Lilies 4

                Later

                                my sister became too ill

for the clinical trials

                                                but there was a tease

                around Easter

                                        we could still

        hope, more will

                                than possibility, a straw

                                                        false lease

                        I began to tell

                                        her about the Water Lilies

watched her stare

                at each panel as if I

                                        were a merchant unfolding my wares

            to make them so real

                                so *literal*

                                        she might climb the tiers

        of painted air the way lilies

                                rise

                                        out of shit and silt

    So Monet writ

                his "terrible blizzard of loss that will

                                                even erase

    her features" John Berger writes

                                of the portrait of his young wife's wrestle

        with death; saw

                        painted light unlike the real

is not transparent—more a wall

                        and she, now, a corpse on an easel

Water Lilies 5

the air's alert

 a Parisian jumps at the least

 sound, it's the law

 of hatred, rule of Ares

 sewer of ire

 a weary aisle

of fear, the stairwell

 climbs down or up its

 own dark rails

 Fear has a long lease

 retails

 see it in the child's welts

 the wallets

 of suffering and riot

 suffering in the east

the west

 What is an iris

 to that? A lily? A star?

 A sweet

 roll from the now-dark café? It's

the last straw

 a waiter (writer)

 says (in French); Ariel's

 attack of fear; he wears

 he says, a sweater

of refugees, the late

 bombed-out sites

The aria

 of war

 je suis allé

 he says, why write?

Water Lilies 6

like straw

in a storm, you are still

at the least

provocation, aswirl

almost real

like the water

Monet painted   what we can't see

then the lilies

like coins spilling out of water

trees, will-

ows, bent at the waist

hair falling, weeping trees

air and water

water and air

and you, sister, still

reel after reel

against all laws

aswirl

Water Lilies 7

suddenly welts

weals, wrestle

onto my skin, a series

of trails

I am my own walls

my body's rash atelier

rails

something writes

from *inside*, tells

retells

my sister dragging the tail

of her oxygen tank; the weariest

days, shadows, trees

ills swell

nothing to erase

nothing to ease

I come to the wall

and the wall

all welter, swells

Water Lilies 8

Clear morning with will-

              ows that will

                       never wilt

leaves, water-

        plants, lilies

open like wallets

         and wars

                 Who tallies

who reels in the literal

        corpses? It's the law

of will

        art of waste

                  the world reels

late stars wobble on the easel

(Water Lilies Floating)

water

                                      lilies

will

             air   wait

air

                iris

                      air

east

              wars

                        water

    teals

                              west

            wisteria

                    trees

   write   air

               water

        will-   lilies

laws

                      ows swirl

   aisle

            air

               reels

;

Deleted Scene: Bargaining (.56)

Here I come again
with my *abra*
cadabra, my gang
of language, to beg,
harangue. Oh Divine Airbag,
I stand here in your rabid Niagara,
with nothing but prayer's ragbag
incantations. Need me to gin
up? Watch me, mere gnat,
up the ante: I'll take the angina,
you take the brain
cancer. My loss is your gain!
Leave me elbow-deep in
your whole grab-bag
of disaster. But bring
her back.

Woman on Cell Phone Dragging an Empty Cart
Through Washington Square Park

It's called Sisyphus. No. *Sisyphus.* Yes. Apparently
some Greek myth. This guy is punished for—*punished*—yes—
for something, and has to roll a rock up a hill every day

and every day it rolls—a rock, yes—
and every day it rolls back down.
Something about the absurdity of life.

Camus says—*Camooo*—says it's
about the condition of man and that
it's meaningless and we have to just keep

doing it and—the rock, yes, rolling the rock—and that
gives our life meaning. Yeah. Well
if that don't drive you to God—

Point-of-View Shot: Celeriac

I can smell it from the living room—tenement yellow, medusa roots
snaking out of bruised bone, the muslin color of mummy wrap—
climbing the flights with its own sweating fever.

I had no idea what it would look like, I just ordered a taste I'd tasted:
sweet, greenish. Not this snaggled hood of twisted reaching, waving
its withered flippers, like those smirking skulls in fetid caves—

what you are now we used to be, what we are—cryptic
cartloads of stiff friars posed with their scythes and plaques, poised
like noisy Day of the Dead dioramas—playing Scrabble or shaving,

binge-watching a TV drama: a girl snarling into her own horror,
grabbing out of her grave, carried in a boatload of the dead, its awful
oars rowing past an ancient city, where, beside one dig, a pious cleric

lifts a goblet that will one day sit on a shelf—just another relic
in a damp museum with its graveyard promise, its mass of gaping griefs.
I look into its eyes, lift it to my lips—earthy, humid—I can see

it will smush to a grimace like a ten-day Halloween pumpkin before
I touch it again. An unsung, many-eyed maniac waving its ridiculous fins.

Trying to Understand Irony

Even the harbors are ironic,
I said in my dream, leaning

over the side of a ship into two bodies
of water, a kind of map, the word "harbor"

sort of lapping back at me. This morning
my home page says I can watch

a teenager interview a prisoner
in Guantanamo. I hit play.

The safety of this life, a pop-up advises,
cannot be determined.

Is this ironic? What is ironic?
Sam asks from his crib. Well, I say,

those pajamas are ironic. I point
to the explosion of planets and stars,

the rock and tumble of spaceships and fusions
he is wearing to bed. How can he sleep

while those stars wobble across his tiny body?
Oh, he says, already sleeping.

My Child

Then I carry you, sleeping, out of the quiet
car seat (we've been driving all night,
traffic, no traffic, the indecipherable
signs and storms, roadside accidents,
your breathing and dream speech)
up the dark stairs, and place you, sleeping,
in your crib. My girl, I say,
or my boy, depending on my mood. Sometimes
I speak to you in Chinese, though I know only
hello and three numbers, sometimes
in show tunes, semicolons.
I tell you what it is to be childless
to listen for you across supermarket aisles
(what trouble I had buckling you into that tiny seat!)
to study your face on milk cartons, worry
about your tests, your fevers. Sooner or later
you'll come crooning into my bedroom.
In every kitchen of the city, your socks and vigor.
Last night slicing fingerling potatoes it occurred
to me I'd left you somewhere. On the subway?
In that shopping cart?

Tracking Shot: Subway Lines

Are you depressed? Have a disability?
Need a divorce? Are you haunted?
Do not lean on ample time,
others will think you are a target.
Flying through history? Everyone wants to
hog poles, find New Lots. Everyone
wants an emergency exit. Are you at risk?
Dog tired? Pregnant? Everyone wants to look
their best, step up, stand out, be held
by the dispatcher. If you see something, say
a clipping, the past, an alarm will sound
like a true story but we think
the soul is primping, seamless, anyway
you swipe it. Just like regular people
in Wakefield. See someone at risk? Remember
you can cook when you're dead. It's a temporary
ferry, a film festival, an express to Gravesend, so always
watch the devices, keep personal gaps
personal. Do not. Do not. Do not. Hold on.

The Blob

I'm a blob, our mother used to say, pregnant again with that
blobby wobble. We had siblings. We knew how a blob became a baby,
the mother bulb oozing out another child, and now there are four

and it's Steve McQueen Week on the *4:30 Movie, The Blob*
ending with its ominous question. *The End?* This was before
I understood irony. We'd seen the drunk old man

prod the ooze and disappear, watched it grow and roll, the little dog
barking its warning . . . barking, barking, then the barking stops
and the blob rolls on, insistent, engulfing the doctor.

We'd seen his face as the thing he didn't believe in—
what has already absorbed his nurse—came over him.
Town after town it rolls, amassing citizens. Now it is itself

a mass. A malignant mindless mob. How do you fight a blob?
Nobody believes Steve, the blob oozing
under the diner door, past the revolving pies.

His name was Steve in the movie and Steve in real life,
cigarette pack rolled in the shoulder of his T-shirt sleeve.
Desire oozed through me. I don't remember how the horror was contained.

Of the ending I remember the question. My sister and I
screaming in the living room, as the horror that was our mother
said, only a movie horror . . . *ended?* 4:30 afternoons.

We'd seen *Dark Shadows.* Seen the way the dead
past comes back, eats you alive. The future will find a mass
in my sister's lung. Size of an orange? Why not say size of a grenade?

Sometimes my childhood closes over me—
enormous, hypnagogic, and I am the crowd
trapped in one of those neon diners of the sixties,

the mob rolling, a bloated demagogue, as now, waiting
in the neighborhood cheese shop, a man's red hands lifting
the rennet and curd out of the boiling

salt and steam, I see my mother, the typeface oozing
down the title screen, my mind, thoughts, nothing
but blob blob blob. The billionaire politician blobbing

across front pages, TV screens, rolling through towns.
Mindless, deadly, malignant. Amorphous, devouring monster.
Why didn't we laugh? Why didn't it seem, well, cheesy?

Surely the director snickered. Surely Steve/Steve understood
it was made of tinted silicone. This happens in sci-fi:
the ordinary nodule transforms into a race of aliens. You're next,

a woman barks. You're next, the crowd shouts. The man with red hands
scowls. Step up. They're late. They want their cheese.
It's only cheese. Why am I so frightened?

Split Screen

<table>
</table>

Scene: Two times, two sisters,   two sets, two spies.
Present: one sleeps, one ripens.   Past: one watches the other creep.
Listen, however unlike their lines   each might be the other's stencil.
It depends on the lens. Précis: on one screen, the I,
tense as a pencil,   is, in the one script,
sinner, the other I splices,   edits its replies.
Clips of spite lie   inert as a relic.
Reel after reel, tireless   each (center) sister
eclipses, splinters   her specter; it's, in a sense,
epic   this urge to lie,
nest in a sister (the center)   unseen

Migraine

             Imagine
Hildegard in her German
          abbey, her visions of "sweet rain"
                 mere mirage;
          nausea, aura, nerve storms ring-
                            ing her brain's rim;
               particles of light rain
     the way grain showers gold in grim
                    tales. No margin.
                              No genii
          her dove in the lattice? No halo?
                       Just a "phosphine rain"
          "disorder of arousal," anger
                  not prayer. Mosaic of rage.
               Pain ramming
     her mind's screens. Imagine
                    the domed panes of the Gare
          d'Orsay before art and enigma
                  replaced the trains. God? Mirage?
               No savior to the manger
                       the migraine pulls in.

Deleted Scene: Last Day

I hear a book being written, my sister says, or is it a poem?

Her eyes are closed.

It has a *lot* of semicolons.

One sentence or two? she wants to know. Comma? Period?

Well, I say, semicolons join *and* separate.

Grammar, my sister says, is very interesting.

Revolve

back to the time we watched the watches revolve
in their revolving case, Mr. Webster watching over
in his drugstore smock and oily leer
for us to choose—say *yes! stop! now!*—then press the lever
so *our* watch stopped and hung,
                            a Ferris wheel's highest rider rocking over
Coney Island. *I can stop time, dollface*; he'd say, every time, and revel
in his scratchy smock. Not once did we ever
buy a watch. I knew we'd leave with Aqua Velva or
Old Spice (the present for our father). Now watch time's reel
spool back along its creaky wheel past fifth grade, third, first and veer
back down the chart of apes that straightened to our fathers. (Where was Eve?)
How right it seemed. I'd dreamed my father was a bear or
some fur-covered thing. Now Mr. Webster was an ape. O
all the world reduced to ore and roe
and nothing but what came before slimy eel
and horny vole. There Mr. Webster rove
the weedy grasses—grabbing at some girl. *Olé! Olé!*
Ah the world goes round and still Mr. Webster in his starring role:
King Kong, hairy-handed lover
grasping a girl, watching her shriek and reel
under his eely leer (*I can stop time, dollface*) forever.

Scary Movie

It was the future we watched—ferocious
pointy-headed, soon-to-be-rerun invaders
colliding out of alien stars with medieval fevers

and no-way-out jousting. Or Stone Age savages
roaring out of the past, with their brontosaurus breath
ripping femurs, shredding flesh like the orange piranha

macerating a puppy in my dream last night.
Perhaps you don't have such dreams.
Perhaps you've never been savage yourself,

never let savagery rip through you
like a cleaver through meat. But what about
what you said to your sister, on the steps of that

kindergarten. That was savage. You knew,
didn't you? You felt it, didn't you feel it
at your desk, minutes later? Her fear

in your gut as you raised your hand, raced past
the cafeteria—boiling greens, groping
cutout hands. They knew what I'd done.

I can't not have done it now.

Washing Her Hair

I warm the lather
in my palm,

dampen the fine, last
strands—all she has

left—to encourage
the suds, then

rinse, fold them
over my hand

(the way I'll hold
the fading paper

wreath she
made in first grade,

and lay it in its box)
and brush,

from the ends up,
gently, so as to lose

not one strand.

A Gate

I have oared and grieved,
grieved and oared,
treading a religion
of fear. A frayed nerve.
A train wreck tied to the train
of an old idea.
Now, Lord, reeling in violent
times, I drag these tidal
griefs to this gate.
I am tired. Deliver
me, whatever you are.
Help me, you who are never
near, hold what I love
and grieve, reveal this green
evening, myself, rain,
drone, evil, greed,
as temporary. Granted
then gone. Let me rail,
revolt, edge out, glove
to the grate. I am done
waiting like some invalid
begging in the nave.
Help me divine
myself, beside me no Virgil
urging me to shift gear,
change lane, sing my dirge
for the rent, torn world, and love
your silence without veering
into rage.

Deleted Scene: Last Day

I'm sorry, my sister says. I'm sorry it's taking so long.

You must be bored to *death*.

Elegy for a Church-Key

(Setsuko Hara, 1920–2015)

When Setsuko Hara sips a beer
in *Early Summer* (or *Late Spring*)
in that static tatami shot, we know she's going
to tip the balance, leave her father.

It's early summer or late spring.
Barbecue days, years before the ring-tab.
My father leaves his cigarette balanced on a can.
Ashes fizz the dregs of beer.

Years before the ring-tab, barbecue years.
The church-key of childhood cracks open the can.
Ashes fizz the dregs of beer.
My father opens a beer, ghosts foam the holes.

A film can cracks: a church-key childhood opens.
I *like* beer, Noriko says. (I've seen this before.)
Ghosts open beers, fathers foam the holes.
Those fathers are gone. The church-keys lost.

I've seen this before, Noriko says.
(Her name is Noriko in both of these movies.)
The church-key is lost. That father gone.
Loss is loss, what matters the movie?

Her name is Noriko in both of these movies
Setsuko Hara still sipping her beer.
Loss is loss, what matters the movie?
Nothing is static in a tatami shot.

Trailer

[*Some Language, Some Death, Some Prayer, Some War*]

FADE IN:

INT. LIVING ROOM—DAY

A couch. Table with medications, tissues, cough drops. A TV

> VOICE-OVER
> In a world of . . .

DISSOLVE TO:

INT. HOSPITAL WAITING ROOM—INDETERMINATE TIME

Men and women on couches. Table with coffee urn, tea, graham crackers. A TV

Philip Glass music UNDER. TV news UNDER.

A woman, holding a tissue, walks to the table.

> WOMAN
> Do you want decaf?

CUT TO:

INT. CHURCH—DAY

Statue of Virgin Mary overlooking rows of lit candles.

Philip Glass music UNDER. Praying voices UNDER.

> VOICE-OVER
> Based on the true story of . . .

DISSOLVE TO:

INT. BED BATH & BEYOND—DAY

Aisle of glass containers. A woman wheels a cart.

VOICE-OVER
Will she find it in time?

CUT TO:

INT. DOCTOR'S OFFICE—DAY

Room lit by overhead fluorescent. Woman seated on examination table.
Man and Woman standing on either side.

VOICE-OVER
Featuring the award-winning star of
"Third Grade" and "Christmas at Nanna's"

CUT TO:

INT. KITCHEN—NIGHT

One light on. Two women, one seated. Camera lingers on them then
PANS TO a CLOSE-UP of a clock. 3:10.

CUT TO:

EXTREME CLOSE-UP of one woman's face.

Philip Glass music UNDER.

CUT TO:

CLOSE-UP of clock. 3:14

VOICE-OVER
In a shocking twist, the . . .

CUT TO:

Marginalia

I love to find a stranger's marker limn
the margin of some argument—a girl,
I imagine, trapped in a grim
assignment, my sister, perhaps, arm
dangling over the bed edge trying to nail
the main point, beating the sluggish animal
of her attention, asleep again,
me opposite, her anagram,
more rearrangement than mirror, a gnarl
of complaint, hitched to some grail
far from her as now I limn
her words in the margin
of Kierkegaard: *no justice to be found in
the physical world.* Her words? Rag
of some teacher's gloss? Inscrutable mail
from my dear one two months dead.

;

Bird-Watching

Perhaps it's habit,

           an itch

    for God, this watching—

               heart? spirit?— dart

   twist, braid

       itself into a chain

              of waiting.

  You can't drag

         spirit, force a hatch,

 but must wait—

      no branch

  to grab. No rag

       to wring.

You must abide.

      Abide?

         O heart, hang

  on your twig,

      rant

        your raw song.

Something's taken wing.

      Some bandit

  left me this grid of rain.

;

Notes

"The Extra": Quotes are from *The Tibetan Book of Living and Dying*.

"The Port": This poem began as my response to Diane Seuss's initial stanza in a sestina contest judged by David Lehman for *The American Scholar*.

"Movie" is for my brother Gregg Masini.

"Water Lilies": This series was inspired by Monet's *Les Nymphéas* in the Musée de l'Orangerie, Paris. John Berger quotes are from his essay "Claude Monet."

"Tracking Shot: Subway Lines": This collage of phrases is made out of signs and ads in a subway car.

"Migraine": In his study *Migraine*, Oliver Sacks explores the phenomenon as both neurological structure and emotional strategy, a cinematographic series of flickering stills being one of its many sensory manifestations. Hildegard of Bingen (1098–1179) was a Benedictine mystic, composer, visionary, and scientist.